Sister Sage's Astrological Journeys

AS ABOVE, SO BELOW

Reverend Rhonda Schienle

Interfaith Ministry Services, LLC
Valparaiso, IN

Copyright © 2017 by Rhonda Schienle.

All rights reserved. No part of this publication may be reproduced, distributed or transmitted in any form or by any means, including photocopying, recording, or other electronic or mechanical methods, without the prior written permission of the publisher, except in the case of brief quotations embodied in critical reviews and certain other noncommercial uses permitted by copyright law. For permission requests, write to the publisher, addressed "Attention: Permissions Coordinator," at the address below.

Rhonda Schienle / Interfaith Ministry Services, LLC
236 Southwind Dr.
Valparaiso, IN 46385
www.interfaithministryservices.com

Book Layout ©2017 BookDesignTemplates.com

Ordering Information:
Quantity sales. Special discounts are available on quantity purchases by corporations, associations, and others. For details, contact Interfaith Ministry Services, LLC at the address above.

This book is not intended as a substitute for the medical advice of physicians. The reader should regularly consult a physician in matters relating to his/her health and particularly with respect to any symptoms that may require diagnosis or medical attention.

Sister Sage's Astrological Journeys / Rhonda Schienle. —1st ed.
ISBN-13: 978-0-998-84060-4
ISBN-10: 0-998-84060-2

Contents

Dedications v

Gratitude to my Loving Animals vii

About this Book...viii

Patterns, Themes, Rhythms and Symbols........................1

    Karma 2

Dragon's Head and Tail 5

Retrograde 9

Luminary Keywords and Symbols 11

    Sun 11

    Moon 11

Planet Keywords and Symbols 13

    Mercury 13

    Venus 13

    Mars 14

    Jupiter 14

    Saturn 14

    Uranus 15

    Neptune 15

    Pluto 16

Zodiac Keywords and Symbols 17

    Aries 17

    Taurus 18

    Gemini 19

    Cancer 20

    Leo 21

    Virgo 22

    Libra 23

    Scorpio 24

    Sagittarius 25

    Capricorn 26

    Aquarius 27

    Pisces 28

Housing System 29

    Housing System Chart 29

    Housing System Wheel 30

Natal Chart 31

Forecast: Dragon's Head & Tail 32

Dragon's Head in Leo and Tail in Aquarius 32

Dragon's Head in Leo 34

Dragon's Tail in Aquarius 36

Famous People born in August or February 37

People born in August 39

People born in September 40

People born in October 42

People born in November 43

People born in December 44

People born in January 45

People born in February 46

People born in March 48

People born in April 49

People born in May 50

People born in June 51

People born in July 52

Forecast: Saturn in Sagittarius 54

Forecast: Uranus in Aries 57

Keywords for Uranus/Aquarius/February 58

Keywords for Aries/Mars/April 59

Forecast: Neptune in Pisces 64

Keywords for Neptune/Pisces/March 64

Forecast: Pluto in Capricorn... 67

Pluto in Capricorn Generation 68

Previous history for Pluto in Capricorn 73

Closing statement 75

About the Author 76

Dedications

Mike Schienle

Thank you my darling husband, whom I call Love Bug, for being my best friend in the whole world. You are a witness to my life; through the hills and the valleys, trials and triumphs with amazing grace and love in your heart. I am eternally grateful to God for you. My heart is filled with joy that you are my love, friend and biggest fan.

http://www.customvisuals.com/

Marsha Marcoe

Thank you for your care, compassion and support during some of the hardest times in my life. From the deepest place in my heart, there could have been no other person to gift me with healing my spirit and empowering my soul. This phrase has become my living and working mantra.

http://www.marshamarcoe.com/

Louis Turi Astrologer

I will be forever grateful, Louis, for your generous time in training those who already had the calling to become an AstroPsychologist. Thank you for rekindling the method of "Divine Astrology" and sharing your gifts with the world.

Scott Grossberg

Thank you for your amazing book "The Most Magical Secret: 4 weeks to an Ecstatic Life" that has inspired and encouraged me to move forward with my passions, dreams and to live an ecstatic life. With your guidance and wisdom, I have reclaimed my Magic!

http://www.thinkingmagically.com/

Ron Papke

Ron, I thank you for encouraging and inspiring me to put the time back into my passions and callings. To demonstrate through your own actions how to set a goal with a time commitment and achieve it; has made a big impact on my life. Your books "Create Yourself" and "How to Write a Book" are an inspirational gift to many.

https://www.ronpapke.com/

David Chastain

To an amazing, gifted and kind artist in this world, I thank you for your zodiac drawings and my windfall logo. These images have touched my spirit for more than 18 years now.

http://www.10000things.com/

Gratitude to my Loving Animals

Samantha
Our kitty, who loved when mommy sang to her. We miss you.

Tinkerbelle
Our prancing, princess kitty who stole our heart from a store window and hid toys in our shoes. We miss you.

Malone
Our Rottweiler dog, our son. We were humbled to have had you in our lives. We miss you.

Jingles
Our funny, crazy German Shepherd and Rottweiler mix, what a joy it was to watch you play. We miss you.

Squirt
Our cuddling kitty. You came into our lives at a poignant time. Thank you for finding and choosing us as your mommy and daddy.

Lily Adele
Our sweet, adventurous, photo bombing kitty, funny and so loved. Mommy and Daddy hit the jackpot when we got you Spunky Monkey.

"He is wise who understands that the stars are luminaries, created as signs. He who conquers the stars will hold the golden keys to God's mysterious universe."

~ Nostradamus

About this Book

The title of this book comes from a nickname given to me many years ago. My passion for all things different have given me many funny nicknames, but "Sister Sage" really stood out for me. There was some humorous truth to it. When I signed off of a reading or prediction, I would write, "Safe Astrological Journeys". And now we have the title of my book.

This book is not about training on how to use the method of Astrology discussed, as much as it is to observe, notice and feel what is being shared. If it is information that resonates, that is wonderful.

What is being shared is a method of Astrology I learned many years ago called "Divine Astrology". Simply put this is a method which requires no mathematical equations or deep astrological understandings.

I incorporate, not only the training I took on this astrology method, but my personal experiences, educational background and professional working environments. One element that I have found to be very helpful to astrological forecasting or interpreting is using your intuition. Another is, always use your own best judgment and discernment.

I enjoy astrology, quantum physics, law of attraction and other various metaphysical endeavors. Over the years I enjoyed having astrological readings done. Always listening to the New Year predictions on television talks shows. It was fascinating to see what would come of those predictions.

Then, one day I listened to someone on the radio who did professional astrology readings. I was intrigued and had those same questions. How does he know this and how does this really work?

Later, I noticed he had a training course and study program, I immediately signed up. I completed my training and received my certificate in December of 1999. From there I enjoyed a few years of doing astrological readings as a business and have my website KarmicLaw.com to this day. I still do some readings and forecasting here and there, and love every minute of it.

What I enjoy about this particular method is the the underlying concept. If you can remember what birth month someone is born in, that is what begins the cycle of their birth chart. Okay, I can remember that, I thought. Regardless of the day one is born, just remember the birth month and all the keywords, symbolism and meaning of that given month. This knowledge will be helpful when you read the chapters on "Forecasting."

CHAPTER 1

Patterns, Themes, Rhythms and Symbols

Our ancient ancestors were not using software or programs back in the day, but looked up to the heavens and could easily see what was above in star formations. It didn't take humans long to realize when the seasons were changing. There were noticeable patterns.

We can stand at the beach and notice when the tides begin to turn. It is quite rhythmic. We do not have to remind the ocean when it is high or low tide. We can observe the Sun coming up or going down and notice the change in hours we have of daylight as the seasons change.

Isn't it also interesting to notice that our lives have similar patterns, themes or rhythms? Our heartbeats have a rhythm and cadence. This applies to our sleeping patterns and how we breathe. In addition, many of us admit repeating the same human patterns over and over again, either in relationships or behavior.

As an example, I have met people who tend to attract the same abusive love partner or personalities they deem as narcissistic. Another example is living the theme from a victimhood standpoint.

Then there is symbolic or symbolism that expresses other elements in life. When we go to pick out a wedding ring for our love partner and go before a minister or wedding officiant and they describe the symbolic meaning of the ring. One of the phrases commonly used about the wedding ring is that it is made in a complete and perfect circle, with no beginning or end. Is this to state that our love is never ending? Does it intimate that we are two complete people uniting as one?

I'm fascinated by themes, patterns, rhythms and symbolism in life. I have been studying, observing and learning over the years the concept of natural laws. Some refer to this as laws of nature. No one can make changes to these phenomena, for they are not man made. As I shared earlier, there are noticeable patterns in these phenomena.

One of the most popular ones is Karma. I have done talks about the Law of Karma in a church service and for my Spiritual Laws, Theories and Practices group. At first we giggle at the question, how many of you believe in karma? Yes, almost the entire room raises their hands and recognizes the truth in this natural law. We inherently know that the saying of, "What goes around, comes around" exists.

Even in scripture it is noted, "What you sow, so shall you reap." Have you ever seen what a boomerang does? You throw it out and it comes back to you.

Why does this natural phenomena occur? Do you love my questions? I want you all to be empowered, think, feel and observe to find your answers. So too in scripture as it says, "Ask, and ye shall receive."

Karma

I get a variety of questions about all aspects of a person's chart or upcoming forecast, and often answer, "It depends." They ask me, "Depends on what?" My reply is simply, "Your Karma!" What have you done in these areas or departments of your life in the last 18 years or are you using your innate gifts to the greater good of all? Every sign and symbol offers you a choice of how you are going to use their influences: good, bad, right, wrong.

I further share, what you have put into something is proportionate; meaning exactly what you will get out of it. As Newton's Third law of Motion states: "For every action, there is an equal and opposite reaction."

Those who go to medical school, study hard, complete all their training and internship know their effort is proportional to what they will ultimately receive. Speaking of education, have you noticed others who have a pattern of starting something and not completing it and then get upset at the outcome? If this is a pattern they recognize and it's in their awareness, they can begin to make the changes.

These types of patterns, rhythms and themes can show up in our astrological charts, too. What is exciting about the astrological chart is it can help you look at where some of your patterns might show up and in what areas of your life, so you can work with it and manage it better. Remember this, you always have choice. You have the choice to make a course correction or behavior change. Much like those fun bumper cars at a theme park. If you hit one side of the track, it bounces you back to the middle. This is a great visual for me.

We are like kids on the planet and when we get out of line or alignment, the universe wants to course correct us. It is there to help and assist, not punish. Some people believe this understanding of Karma is bad. Not so. If you send out kindness, that is what is returned. Working to the greater good of all people is what I like to work and live by. Perhaps Karma is the natural educational system.

Okay, I digress.

With symbols, it applies in astrology, too. Much like the stop signs we see on the road. They have meaning and messages. Hopefully we all know what "stop" means! The symbol for each zodiac sign, for example, has its own meanings, elements and properties. When we get to that chapter, I will share those and some corresponding keywords for each one.

Another important area of this book is the term, cycle. In the coming chapters I will mention cycles of planets or grouping of zodiac signs. They are cyclic in the sense that they will return to a department in your life every so many days, months or even years.

A final mention and highly important is that the planets and luminaries do no discriminate against anyone or anything. They are divinely created, therefore, no mistakes. Onward! Let's journey further.

"Life is a mirror and will reflect back to the thinker what he thinks into it."

~ Ernest Holmes

CHAPTER 2

Dragon's Head and Tail

There are different names for the Dragon's Head and Dragon's Tail. Some refer to the Dragon's Head as the North Node of the Moon, both implying luck. The Dragon's Tail is also referred to as the South Node of the moon, indicating past life or restructure. The significance in each of these is the Dragon's Head and Tail in one's natal or birth chart indicates many things.

One is how the person is to learn, develop and attain in this lifetime. Yes, I said this lifetime. Reincarnation is mentioned here. Like mentioned in the above paragraph, it gives the energy of luck. The other aspect to the Dragon's Head is to know which house it resides in. For example, does it sit in the house of home and family or career area?

The Tail of the Dragon is where we came from in past life. It's other name is karmic residue. It also reflects the type of energies, patterns or residual effects we might be carrying over into this lifetime. Much like a 401K rollover. Humor! The Dragon's Tail can test us, because even if it is subconscious we might be doing something that resembles sliding back to what is familiar or comfortable. The idea is to be challenged and move toward the Dragon's Head for spiritual and soul growth and human evolution. Now wasn't that a powerful statement?

Some of us are not content, but complacent. We get comfortable with the familiar. Can you see how some of the cycles or patterns of behavior can be brought into our lives as I mentioned in the chapter on patterns? As mentioned, the Dragon's Head and Tail when we are born is giving us insight and clues as to where we came from, so to speak, in past life and where we are to head or aim toward in this lifetime. Now, keep in mind that all planets are in motion. So every 18 months or so, the Dragon's Head and Tail will move into two new astrological signs. Therefore, when we are born, we are given what is called our Natal Dragon's Head and Tail. For example, The Dragon's Head in Gemini and the Dragon's Tail in Sagittarius. I will explain these more later on.

These are referred to as opposing signs. Think of it more as your car battery. You have a positive and negative charge on the battery. You need both to make the spark. With these signs, I tend to use the concepts of what gives us our Soul growth, change, life course correction, opportunities and challenges in life.

So we have the Dragon's Head and Tail when we are born and every 18 months it goes into the next two opposing signs in the Universe. What this means is that we need to take a look at where the Dragon's Head and Dragon's Tail are residing in this moment, to determine how it is affecting our world in a larger view then our own personal charts. Then we can ask, how or what areas of my life is this current Dragon's Head or Dragon's Tail affecting my personal chart? When I say current, where it resides today.

I will be forecasting on this a bit later and this will offer a great example of how this works and operates. Another very important element when forecasting or looking at the Dragon's Head is to see when it last entered those two signs. This is significant, because when I give readings I will ask what was happening in your life 18 years ago. Yes, 18 years not months for this part. It takes 18 years roughly to make a complete revolution to come back around to the same two signs.

Now for me, thankfully I am old enough to look back on 18 years. So I can say what was happening on various levels of my life at that time. This information is relevant to the current meaning right now. It is also very insightful and helpful, much like a review process. It is like a gauging mechanism to see your own spiritual and soul growth.

You can also give yourself a litmus test, by asking these questions: What was happening during those specific dates of the Dragon's Head and Tail? What areas of my life was it affecting? For instance, was I moving, in school, getting married and other similar type of life questions.

An important question is have I learned lessons from whatever was happening at that time period? I will actually share one of my examples of this in the forecasting chapter as it relates to a new Dragon's Head and Tail change in the universe.

Example: Dragon's Head is visible below in this chart image. It is the image that looks like a Horseshoe and the upside down horseshoe is the Dragon's Tail. If you look at where it has house 1 and house number 7, you will see those images or symbols.

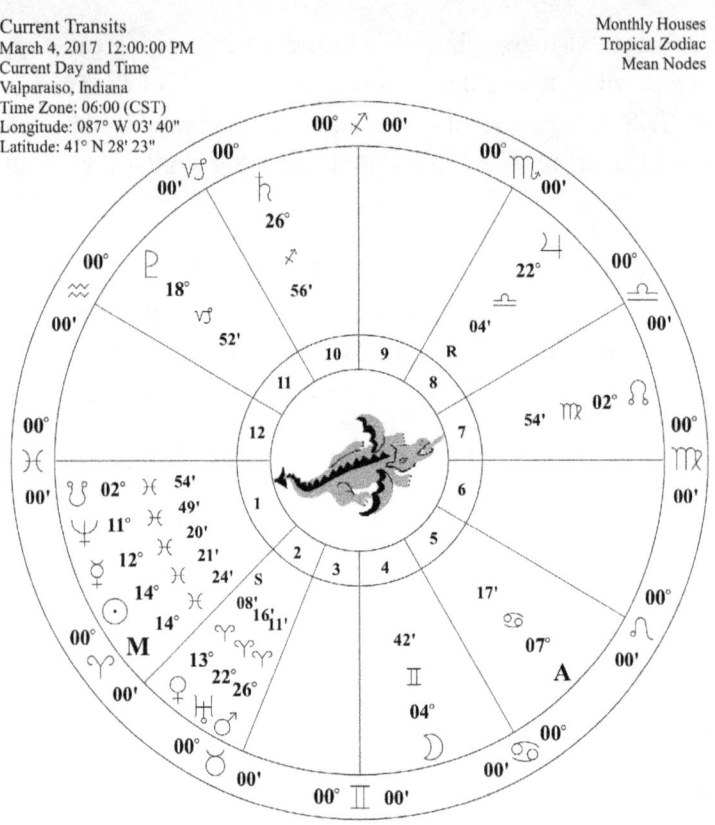

March 4, 2017 Transits

"Every road in life is a journey. The rear view mirror is to remind us of where we have been so that we can fully understand where we are going."

~ Nishan Panwar

Chapter 3

Retrograde

What is retrograde you ask? Some astrologers say that the planet appears to be going in reverse or backwards, relative to the Earth. When this occurs, it is a time to take note, reflect and know that things in your life may not be productive, moving forward or panning out, so to speak.

The most commonly talked about retrograde planet is Mercury. Mercury, in Greek mythology, is the messenger of the gods. It rules communications, reading, writing, schedules, and electronics just to name a few keywords. People on social media platforms are complaining of miscommunication or having to re-schedule their appointments during Mercury retrograde. Also many people claim their batteries quit working in the cars, computers go on the fritz and miscommunication is more heightened during this time. People tend to feel foggy, they say, during a Mercury retrograde time period.

To take this just a little further, there are divine reasons that these phenomena occur. As with Mercury retrograde, the concept is to go within and review what has been happening in your life or reassess what you want to change when Mercury does go direct. It's a time of inner reflection and introspection. I encourage people to actually do a search online when our planets are retrograde. I tend to look them up for each New Year and for each planet. In addition each year I buy an astrological calendar by *Llewellyn*. This helps to plan ahead.

Once you know the meanings of the planets and where that planet resides in your natal chart, then it helps to know how it's affecting you. Remember again, all planets are in motion.

"Nothing happens until something moves."

~ Albert Einstein

Chapter 4

Luminary Keywords and Symbols

Sun

Wherever the Sun is sitting in your chart is where you are to shine, or given opportunities to shine in that area of your life. As with anything else, it also depends of all other influences and planets that are residing in that area of your life that may bring about adversity. Overall, the Sun promotes life and sustenance, have you noticed that? Our vitamin D is produced by exposure to the Sun and brings life to our plants and crops.

Sun governs the sign of Leo. The Sun takes about 30 days in each sign of the zodiac.

Moon

The moon affects us as humans on many different levels. It affects our emotional responses to life. Another is cycles, much like women's menstrual cycles. In nature, it influences our ocean tides and currents, the breeze in the air. Some folks use the moon to determine when to plant their crops or a better time to fish. This can be found in the *Farmers' Almanac*. Ending and beginning phases happen with the moon phases and eclipses. Between the New Moon and Full Moon represents a good time to move forward and sign contracts as a general rule.

Moon governs the sign of Cancer. The moon resides in each zodiac sign about 2.5 days; therefore it takes about 28 days to go through all signs in one full revolution or cycle.

Chapter 5

Planet Keywords and Symbols

Mercury

Mercury in Greek Mythology is called the Messenger of the Gods. This planet affects our communication and expressions. Mercury rules the sign of Gemini.

Keywords: Communication, siblings, reading, writing, radio and telephone.

On average it takes one full year for Mercury to go through a complete revolution through all the zodiac signs. Then, on average, it can go through a sign between 14 to 30 days depending on retrograde motion.

Venus

This planet is considered the Goddess of Love and Beauty. She does like the finer things of life. This planet and its symbol represent the feminine within. Venus is also the planet that pertains to money and personal possessions. Venus governs the signs of Libra and Taurus.

Keywords: Money, beauty, love, real estate.

This planet takes approximately 3 weeks to 2 months depending on the retrograde and direct motions.

Mars

This planet represents the masculine. It is the sign of the hunter and gatherer. Some astrologers have referred to this planet as the Lord of wars. It also represents warriors, motivating entrepreneurs and leaders. Mars governs the sign of Aries.

Keywords: Masculine, War, Desire Principle, Competitive and Leaders

This planet resides in a sign for almost 1.5 months and approximately 2 years to go through a complete cycle of all 12 signs, give or take retrograde motion time.

Jupiter

This planet is typically considered the lucky planet sign. Jupiter governs the zodiac sign of Sagittarius.

Keywords: growth, expansion, opportunities and luck are just a handful of keywords to express this planet. You can read many more keywords when you read the zodiac sign of Sagittarius.

It takes Jupiter approximately 12 months to go through a sign, and about 12 years to go through a complete cycle of all 12 signs.

Saturn

One of the many aspects of Saturn to keep in mind is that it offers structure, discipline and it is karmic in nature. Many astrologers have referred to Saturn as Father Time/Patriarchal. Saturn governs the sign of Capricorn.

Keywords: Teacher, Karmic, Discipline, Methodical and Detailed.

It typically takes Saturn about 2.5 years to pass through each sign, and about 29 years for it to complete the cycle through all 12 signs. You might hear the term, "Saturn Return" when you have astrology readings. This means it has made its full revolution in a particular sign of your natal chart. There is an element of Saturn when looking at charts to determine some karmic residue; meaning where you left off and some areas in your life or chart that can be cleaned up in this lifetime.

Uranus

This planet is one of eccentricity and offers us advancement in so many areas of our life and world. It brings the human race forward. It propels us forward with knowledge, and for the most part, will not allow any form of complacency in our lives. Uranus governs the sign of Aquarius.

Keywords: Awakener, New age, Electrical, Inventions, Aeronautics and Astronomy.

This planet takes approximately 84 years to make a full and complete cycle through each zodiac, and it will remain in a sign for about 7 years.

Neptune

This planet has been referred to as the Greek God of the Seas, also known as Poseidon. Neptune governs the sign of Pisces.

Keywords: Christianity, religion, jails, hospitals, Oceans.

It takes Neptune approximately 165 years to go through all 12 zodiac signs, which equates to about 14 years per sign.

Pluto

As with other planets, there are various meanings and keywords to Pluto. One very important aspect of Pluto is it can be used as generation identification. An example is our baby boomer generation or generation X. Pluto governs the zodiac sign of Scorpio.

Keywords: Death and Rebirth, Regenerate, Mysticism.

It typically takes Pluto approximately 14-30 years for each sign. It takes about 248 years to go through all the signs for a full and complete circle. This lengths of time coincides with generational and historical information.

"The stars dot out the plans of God."

~ James Lendall Basford (1845–1915), Sparks from the Philosopher's Stone, 1882

Chapter 6

Zodiac Keywords and Symbols

Aries

Month: April
Governing Planet: Mars
Symbol: The Ram
Keywords:
Missiles, Ballistics
Fire, Pyrotechnics
Nuclear
Stunt doubles
NATO, Department of Defense
Military, War, Guns
Generals, Warriors, Soldiers
Leadership
Visionaries, Entrepreneurs
Psychologists
Lasers (surgery or otherwise)
Engineers
Football, Boxing, Martial Arts
Steel industry
Metals (copper, iron, silver)
Race car drivers, Automobiles

Medical/Anatomical/Health:
Head, Brain
Eyes, Ears
Geographical locations:
Germany
North Korea
South Korea

Taurus

Month: May
Governing Planet: Venus
Symbol: The Bull
Keywords:
Banks
Swiss bank accounts
Day traders
Financial planners
Massage therapists
Fine art industries
Money
Real estate (homes/property)
Real estate and Property Management firms
Love
Beauty products/industry
Cosmetics
Jewelry
Dancing
Music
Beauty and Spa Salons
Clothing (material possessions)
Home Furniture industries
Medical/Anatomical/Health:
Thyroid
Neck
Upper shoulder areas
Geographical locations:
Switzerland
Cayman Islands

Gemini

Month: June
Governing Planet: Mercury
Symbol: The Twins
Keywords:
Communication, Phones
Speaking, Lecturing
Reading, Writing, Authors
Comedians
Dancing, Music (CD, DVD)
Tires on cars
Automobiles
Department of Motor Vehicles
Drivers Education
Clocks
Phone Companies
Internet
Radio, CB
Video and Film editing
Television and monitors
Public Relations
News Anchors
Phone operators
Books
Railways
Transportation Systems
Buses, Trains, Cab Drivers
Sales workers
DJs
911 dispatch services
Communication devices
Messenger services
Batteries

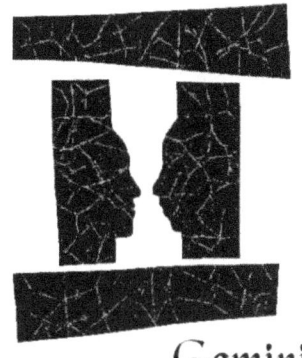

Electrical devices
Electricians
Reiki
Massage Therapy modalities (i.e. touch therapy)
Medical/Anatomical/Health:
Thoughts
Hands
Arms
Lungs
Attention Deficit Disorders
Rationalization
Geographical locations:
New York
Chicago
Boston
Los Angeles
Atlanta

Cancer

Month: July
Governing Luminary: Moon
Symbol: Crab
Keywords:
Emotional
Feminine
Chefs
Cooks (like the Betty Crocker's of cooking/baking)
Real estate agents (Taurus is also real estate)
Day care, Nannies
Care givers
Maids
Meals on Wheels
Foods
Homeless Shelters
Shelters
Feeding/Food
Nurturing
Sensitive
Warmth and love
Nourishment/food
Hotels
Restaurants
Food industries
Cancer (mother)

Medical/Anatomical/Health:
Stomach
Breasts
Female organs
Geographical locations:
United States

Leo

Month: August
Governing Luminary: Sun
Symbol: Lion
Keywords:
Performing Arts
Actors & Actresses
Modeling/Models
Stage productions/Theatre
Movie productions
The Arts in general
Nobel Peace Prize
Teachers for Children
Famous/infamous people
Workers for enlightenment
Sharing/promoting knowledge
Educational Teacher
Famous Researchers in research and development
Famous Athletes
Workers for children's programs

Medical/Anatomical/Health:
The Heart
Geographical locations:
Italy
France

Virgo

Month: September
Governing Planet: Mercury
Symbol: Goddess of Harvest/That of the "Virgin" Mary/Purity
Keywords:
Perfection
Workers in health industry
Critical (self and others)
Analytical
Medical field
Priests, Pastors, Ministers
Medical secretaries
Fitness centers
Weight control organizations
Communications work
Accountants
Beauticians
Farmers
Herbs and plants
Vegan/organic
Seamstress, detailed costume
Clothing making

Medical/Anatomical/Health:
Intestines
Stomach
Abdomen
Elimination process
Geographical locations:
Holland, Netherlands
Large cities

Libra

Month: October
Governing Planet: Venus
Symbol: Scales
Keywords:
Justice department
Justice and injustice
United Nations
Mediation (work and experts)
Harmony
Balance
Diplomats
Lawyers
Justice of the peace
Psychology
Contract agreements
Negotiations
Business partners
Marriage partners
Laws
Universal and man made laws
Astro-Psychology (what you are reading)
Feng Shui
Marriage counselors
Legal secretaries
Paralegals
Legal system (from top down)
Fashion Design
Interior design
Courts
Unions (in organizations)
Tai Chi and related instructors

Medical/Anatomical/Health:
Kidneys
Lymphatic System
Geographical locations:
Switzerland
Cayman Islands

Scorpio

Month: November
Governing Planet: Pluto
Symbol: The Scorpion
Keywords:
IRS, Taxes
Securities Exchange Commission
Federal Trade Commission
Federal Reserve
Welfare System
Loan and finance companies
Banks, Mortgages
Investment firms (i.e. E*TRADE)
Insurance companies
Medicare/Social Security
Surgeons, Surgery centers
Death (literally and metaphorically)
Medical Laboratories
Ob-Gyn Doctors and facilities
Scientists (medical, aerospace, etc.)
Medical Examiners and Offices
Planned Parenthood
Blood (medical) laboratories
Venipuncture workers & equipment
Red Cross Organization
Criminal Investigators
Crime Scene Investigators
Secret Service, CIA
Cold Criminal Case review
Sex (topics, discussion of)
Sex Crime units (police)
Sexual predators
Prostitutes
Detectives, Investigators
Mafia
Russian Spies/Dual agents
Morgues, Funeral Homes
Metaphysics
Death and rebirth
Endings and beginnings
Abortions
Paranormal Investigators
Medical/Anatomical/Health:
Female sexual organs
Male sexual organs
Geographical locations:
Russia

Sagittarius

Month: December
Governing Planet: Jupiter
Symbol: The Centaur
Keywords:
Animals
Kennels
Police, Law enforcement
Firefighters
Football players
Natural/Universal Laws
Naturopathic
Shamans, Light workers/Healers
Horses, Dogs
Wilderness, Forestry work
Nature trails
Veterinary Medicine
Native American Indians
Photography
Publishing, Journalism
Newspapers, Magazines
Sales, Marketing
Landlord/Apartment Managers
Travel Agents, Travel Industries
Tourism
Philosophy, Theology
Teaching or Teachers
Schools, Educational facilities
Mental exploration
Long distance traveling
Foreign Travels and Foreigners
Religion (non-specific)
Ministers and Ministries

Medical/Anatomical/Health:
Lower back
Adipose, Lipids in body
Thighs
Geographical locations:
Australia
Spain
Portugal
Latin American Countries
Southwest US Desert areas
Portions of Egypt, Great Victoria, Sahara, Patagonia areas

Capricorn

Month: January
Governing Planet: Saturn
Symbol: The Goat
Keywords:
Hardware
Electronics
Architecture
Builders (homes-architectures i.e. highways, buildings)
Home Structures
Infrastructures
Real Estate
City Hall Workers
City Officials
Police Officers
Public Service
Architects
Political Fundraisers
Hardware Engineers
Structural Engineers
Psychologists
Governors
Government
Antiques
Ancient Artifacts
Circuit Boards
Life/Home Organizers
Presidential Office
Real Estate Developers
City Planners
Mayors
Governor's
The Karmic Teacher (Saturn)

Frozen Principle
Rigid/disciplined/disciplinarian/authoritarian
Labor intensive
(Father or Father time)
Medical/Anatomical/Health:
Knees
Skeletal system
Teeth
Geographical locations:
England

Aquarius

Month: February
Governing Planet: Uranus
Symbol: Water Bearer
Keywords:
Computers/World Wide Web
Information technology
Social media gadgets
App's for phones
Facebook
Electronics, Electric Grid
Solar Panels, Light Bulbs
Aeronautics, Aviation Industry, Aerospace
Air Force
NASA, JPL
Airplanes, Airlines, pilots
Nuclear devices, missiles
Uranium
Satellites
Star Wars Technology
Paratroopers, skydivers
UFO sightings
Earthquakes, Volcanos
Explosions, Eruptions
Tsunamis from earthquakes
Astronomy, space programs
Inventions, Patents
Scientists, Astrophysics
New age products, devices
Quantum Mechanics, Fractals
Humanitarian, global efforts
Mathematicians

Medical/Anatomical/Health:
Electrical components of body
Autism, Indigo Children
Eccentric
Panic, anxiety attacks
Heart
Geographical locations:
Japan

Pisces

Month: March
Symbol: Fish
Keywords:
Hurricanes
Cinematography
Religion (specific to Christianity)
Oil, Gas industry
Pharmaceuticals
Dream therapies
Oceanography, Oceanographers
Jails
Open seas
Ocean vessels
Hospitals
Insane asylums
Psychiatry wards
Soap Operas
Ballet, Music
Cruise liners
Famous artists,
Paintings, painters
Alcohol industry
Theme Parks
Psychic Mediums
Hypnosis Work
Medical/Anatomical/Health:
Feet
Subconscious
Geographical locations:
Middle East and Hawaii

Chapter 7

Housing System

Housing System Chart

House	Meaning
1st	Innate gifts and abilities, personality, Self, Health
2nd	Self-esteem, material possessions, bank accounts
3rd	Communication, short distance traveling, expression, siblings, critical thinking
4th	Home, family, foundation, Mother
5th	Love, romance, children, creativity, private entertainment
6th	Co-workers, working environment, service to the world, health
7th	Marriage partners, business partners, contracts/agreements, facing the world
8th	Legacy, death and regeneration, corporate monies, investments, inheritances
9th	Higher learning, philosophies, long distance traveling, mental exploration
10th	Career, public standing, achievements, awards
11th	Friends, original experiences, hopes, wishes and dreams
12th	Subconscious, hidden/emotional blocks, accumulation of subconscious memories

Housing System Wheel

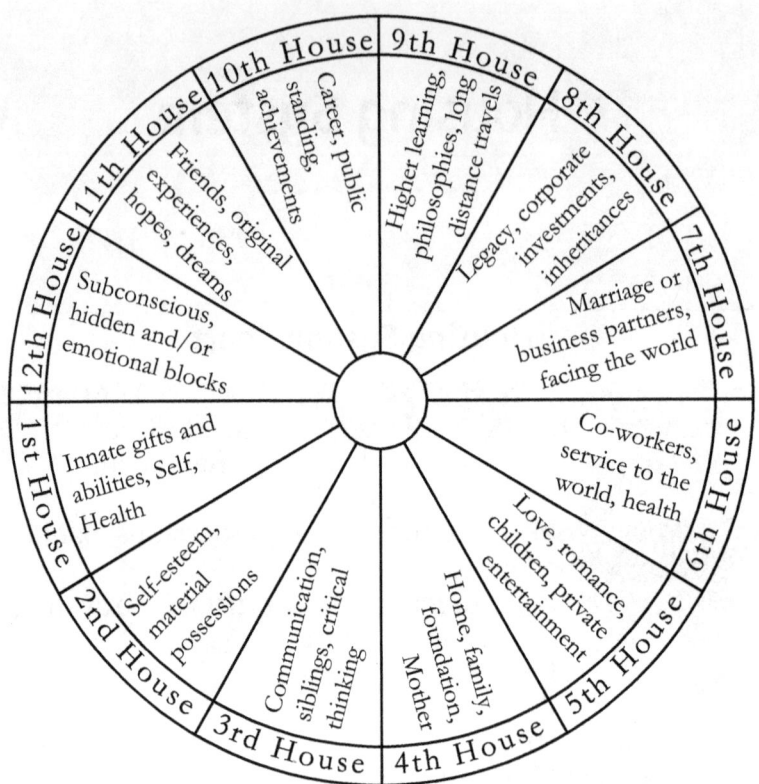

Wheel View of Housing System

CHAPTER 8

Natal Chart

The natal chart also is referred to as the birth chart. When you were born, all the planets, luminaries, asteroids, and, let's just say the cosmos, were in a particular alignment. You inherited these alignments for the date, time and location you were born. How you use these energies and influences is up to you.

I also like to remind people that the planets, luminaries and our world are in motion – literally! So it is important to know when these changes are occurring and in what area of your birth chart it is affecting. Your natal chart has so many characteristics only about you and pertaining to you. Your karma is just an example. Have you had spiritual and soul growth? What lessons were you to attain in a previous life and did you attain them?

When you receive a natal chart, notice that you are all the zodiac symbols. Each house or department on your astrological wheel represents each zodiac sign, Aries through Pisces. This is sharing that you are the sum parts of the whole. You have a part of each zodiac influencing some area of your chart and you. Perhaps this is another way of saying we are all connected.

CHAPTER 9

Forecast: Dragon's Head & Tail

Written February 14, 2017

As mentioned, we have a Dragon's Head and Dragon's Tail that reside in our Natal or Birth chart that will be with us until our physical departure from this earth-plane. Then, as the planets are in motion, approximately every 18 months they will go into 2 new opposing signs. Then, approximately 18+ years it makes its full revolution and returns to the same exact signs.

As mentioned above, I am writing this on February 14, 2017 where the moon is in my 10th house of career. My 10th house of career is Libra.

Dragon's Head in Leo and Tail in Aquarius

The Dragon's Head in Leo and the Dragon's Tail in Aquarius will commence April 28th, 2017 and leave November 15th, 2018. These two signs will be residing for approximately 18 months in Leo and Aquarius respectively.

The last time the Dragon's Head in Leo and Dragon's Tail in Aquarius reigned was September 18th, 1998 to December 31st, 1999. So here is a great example with me as it pertains to this upcoming Dragon's Head in Leo and Tail in Aquarius and the last time it was in those same signs. As I sit here and write this book, the timing is divine and impeccable as it relates to the stars. It is like a full circle moment for me. Why should I be stunned like I feel right now, when I know this information?

I digress.

I was reading another astrologer's site on Facebook recently where she mentioned to understand what is happening now, it would be good to look back at 1999. So, this is where I had to ask myself what was happening back then? My husband and I were living in Lompoc, California around the 1998 and 1999 times mentioned.

These dates of the last Dragon's Head and Tail happen to be around the time when I was listening to the astrologer on the radio and bought the program to learn this type of astrology. My certificate that I received for completing the AstroPsychology course was dated December 16th, 1999.

So, fast forward and here we are again as of this coming April of 2017, where the exact same Dragon's Head and Tail are affecting my 2nd house of money, self esteem, personal property and my 8th house of legacy/life, corporate money, death and rebirth (spiritual and soul growth), and investments.

Now I am writing a book on what subject? Astrology! How is that for cycles, themes and patterns?

I learned a particular type of astrology during the 1998-1999 time period when the Dragon's Head was in Leo and Tail in Aquarius and this is where it is to reside in just 2 months from now. This book will be published when it returns again.

Soul growth? Yes and absolutely! I would have to say my Soul has grown since then with regards to my hobby and passion of astrology.

Dragon's Head in Leo

April 28th, 2017 to November 15th, 2018

All of the industries and geographical areas mentioned in the keywords and meanings chapter will go through major changes and/or restructure during this time frame.

Industries: Dragon's Head in Leo will create changes and restructuring for those who work in acting or performing arts. This is also stage productions and theatre environments. Those who are famous and in the limelight will have more attention brought upon them. I use the term influx to say this will be much more than usual. This means reading it in newspapers, seeing it on television and social media outlets. This change and restructuring can easily range from negotiations to updating their industries to meet the needs of what society is doing and feeling at the time.

Teachers will also make more headlines and be in the news. It is a time with this Dragon's Head and Tail to bring about change as it pertains to what is and is not working. A few examples of this are with tenure, curriculum or performance. In other words, do we keep a teacher who is not performing their teaching duties and remains a teacher due to tenure?

Research and development will make a big comeback during this time frame. The categories range from genealogy, geology and anything to do with precious metals. This includes mining for these various types of metals as well.

Other areas of growth, challenge and change will be with children's programs, new age and enlightenment studies. The growth aspect can be introducing more new age concepts in the traditional educational system or creating more schools that advance spiritual enlightenment.

Geographical: France, Italy. More news will be coming out of these geographical locations. Some will be government changes and challenges. It could show up as upheaval to make these changes or necessary changes. They could go through many changes, challenges and restructuring. This can include economic, government, laws, job market and so forth.

Anatomical: Leo rules the heart. Now, this includes figuratively and literally speaking. On a literal level, we may see an increase of new advances in technology with regards to surgeries or new heart health information. Figuratively speaking, look for ways that the medical or scientific industry measures how emotions or other outer influences affect the heart. Examples are how thoughts or biofeedback mechanisms work with heart matters.

Movies: During the reign of Dragon's Head in Leo we will see an influx of movies that pertain to many famous or infamous people on the movie screen. For some it will be honoring their work or contributions to our world and others will be geared toward famous celebrities and former athletes. Also, since Leo rules France and Italy, we may see more movies made in these locations or about these countries.

News: When I do readings about the change of the next Dragon's Head and Tail, it comes with mentioning that the industries, geographical locations and people in the industries will make headlines in the news more often than usual.

Dragon's Tail in Aquarius

Industries: Computers, NASA, Nuclear plants, Nuclear weapons, Air Force, Planes, Uranium, Missiles and Defense Systems, Astronomy, Electronics, Military, Aerospace, Aviation, Aeronautics, Satellites, International Space Station, Patented or legal licensing, Humanitarian agencies, Astrology and UFO's. All of these industries, and those who work in these industries are going to see changes, restructuring and modernizing.

This energy and combination of Leo and Aquarius Dragon's Head and Tail can lead to more talks and advances in space programs, technology and perhaps planning new space flights. Hearing more about UFO's, stories, witness accounts and even old information coming back to the forefront.

Even though it seems like computer technology changes daily around us anyway, it will become even more advanced. This includes Information technology, inventions, patents and scientific approaches to any new age or hi-tech industry.

The bigger picture here is to take our world and the people in it to a much greater advancement on an enlightenment and technological level. This can bring the human race forward in a much more expansive way. The humanitarian efforts and workers will be in the forefront as well.

Earthquakes, Tsunamis and Volcano's as natural as they are, may see an increase in intensity and or heightened amount of activity.

Geographical: Japan

Anatomical: Heart and Electrical system in the body

Movies: Also since Aquarius rules aeronautics, space programs, inventions or new age products, we can see movies that pertain to these areas and the people who worked in their respective industries.

This includes movies about famous athletes, the industry of sports itself. Who remembers "Back to The Future" movies? This is a great Aquarian and new age type movie. So is the famous "Star Trek" series.

News: We will likely see more news about scientists and major advances with medicines or modalities that relate to the heart as mentioned in the anatomical category; as well as Alzheimer's, Parkinson's, Multiple Sclerosis, Autism and Anxiety disorders. Another area that may see some wonderful advancement is with spinal cord injuries for repairs, new helpful medical equipment and alternative therapies.

The electric companies or electric grid will be getting much more attention or making the headlines. This influence can show up as it is time to make changes, upgrades or updates. After all, Aquarius is about moving the human race forward.

Famous People born in August or February

Remember in the beginning of the book, I mentioned how easy doing this type of astrology is? So for now, regardless of the day a person was born, let's look at their birth month only. Once we determine this, how on a "general" level without seeing the rest of their full birth chart the Dragon's Head and Tail did, or will, affect them. Some of the names below are famous people who have since transitioned to their next journey. For the purpose of astrology, how does their birth month reflect the keywords and traits within the Zodiac signs chapter?

Those born in August (Leo) or February (Aquarius) will be going through major changes, challenges, corrections and restructuring in two specific houses of their life. This will be the first house and seventh house for 18 months beginning April 28th, 2017 through November 15th, 2018.

Famous People Born in August

Name	Date
Steven Wozniak	August 11th, 1950
Fidel Castro	August 13th, 1926
Cameron Diaz	August 30th, 1982
Bill Clinton	August 19th, 1946
Orville Wright	August 19th, 1871
Michael Jackson	August 29th, 1958
Tom Brady	August 03, 1977
Frank Gifford	August 16th, 1930
Barack Obama	August 4th, 1961
Billy Bob Thornton	August 4th, 1961

Famous People Born in February

Name	Date
Steve Jobs	February 24th, 1955
Lisa Marie Presley	February 1st, 1968
Elizabeth Taylor	February 27th, 1932
Thomas Edison	February 11th, 1847
Sheryl Crow	February 11th, 1962
Jennifer Aniston	February 11th, 1962
Jerry Springer	February 13th, 1944
Paris Hilton	February 17th, 1981
Rosa Parks	February 4th, 1913
Harry Styles	February 1st, 1994
Ed Sheeran	February 17th, 1991

People born in August

Your First house Leo: self or innate abilities, physical body or image we project to world.

Seventh house Aquarius: facing the world, contracts, negotiations, mediation and arbitration, marriage partners and business partners.

The Dragon's Head will be in your First house of luck, opportunities.

The Dragon's Tail will be on your Seventh house of restructure, karma and change.

Anyone born in August will be going through major changes, challenges, corrections and restructuring in two specific houses of your life. This will be your first house and seventh house. With this Dragon's Head and Tail in both of these houses will encourage you to either use your gifts, talents further or in different ways. It could bring about new business partnerships, new commitments, contracts or even a new position or title at work. With any change in status of work or business gives you an opportunity to face the world in a different way.

Leo represents working with children, even if they are older than you. It is to promote knowledge, wisdom and life experience to others to further their lives in a better way. If you are in consideration of the performing arts, enlightenment work, working with children or healing arts, the light is green to go.

The Dragon's Head is considered the wheel of fortune and it will be sitting on top of you in your first house of innate gifts and abilities. With this new Dragon's Head and Tail reign it is touching your house of marriage or love partners. This can do both things, either restructures the marriage where there is an imbalance or a new love partner in marriage may be coming in for those single souls born in August. Yes it is true that some marriages end with this combination. Look for those like-minded souls who are born in February as either love partners or business relations.

Also, it is appropriate to take extra time for your overall physical health and find the balance in mind, body and spirit. The term is Self-Care. Since the first house is about Self. Yes, the one with the capital S.

People born in September

Your Twelfth house Leo: subconscious or emotional blocks, hidden from awareness, accumulation of subconscious memories.

Your Sixth house Aquarius: co-workers, working environment, service to the world, health.

The Dragon's Head will be in your Twelfth house of Luck, opportunities and growth.

The Dragon's Tail will be on your Sixth house of restructure, karma and change.

For those born in September this Dragon's Head in Leo and Tail in Aquarius will want to assist and help to bring up those things which have either been dormant or wanting to be brought to your awareness for healing or utilizing a gift. One suggestion with this is to start journaling and writing. Journaling your nighttime dreams is highly encouraged. You are dealing with subconscious memories or hidden thoughts in this house of your chart. By journaling it helps to see if there are any patterns or themes going on. The themes and patterns chapter may need a review to refresh your memory.

The Dragon's Tail may want to restructure your working environment in your sixth house. This can be in many different ways. Either a new job, a new position within your current job, or another way to be of service in your community and world with your gifts and talents.

Your sixth house is in the world of Aquarius. It would be good to go and reference all the keywords in the Zodiac chapter. Sometimes what people do in their career may not necessarily be what they do as their service to community or the world. Your sixth house also refers to your daily health habits and health all together. As the proverbial saying goes; balance and in moderation are key to all aspects of life.

Being born in September try not to over analyze or be too critical of self or others. Instead, use those innate gifts of detail, methodical and organization to the greater good and productive manner.

People born in October

Your Eleventh house Leo: friends, original experiences, hopes, wishes and dreams.

Your Fifth house Aquarius: love, romance, children, creativity, private entertainment.

The Dragon's Head will be in your Eleventh house of luck, opportunities and growth.

The Dragon's Tail will be in your Fifth house of restructure, karma and change.

For those born in October you will see changes and restructure in your eleventh and fifth houses. The Dragon's' head in your eleventh house really wants to see you experience new ideas, groups of people and areas of life differently. It's much like a new adventure and exploring. Those hopes, dreams and aspirations you've wanted to experience are waiting for your attention. Especially look for those friends born in August.

This also can elicit or encourage more of your creative side since your fifth house is going through a restructure and change during this time frame. Those things that pertain to new age endeavors are one of many areas that is being emphasized in your fifth house. Having Aquarius in your fifth house may also encourage you to get involved in humanitarian efforts, support one or create one.

If you are single this Dragon's Head and Tail can bring about a new love partner, where romance can flourish, especially with those born in February. Those that are married and born in October, this can bring about change and restructuring. This does not always mean divorce. It's another cycle of time in the relationship that goes through a change or challenge.

With regards to your eleventh house of friends, be mindful as you grow, sometimes your friendships change too. There will be some who remain in your life while others tend to drift away.

For those born in October and have children, this represents your offspring. This can offer you anything from having a new child, one leaving off to college or getting married. What you offer your offspring dwells in the world of Aquarius.

People born in November

Your Tenth house Leo: career, public standing, achievements, awards.

Your Fourth House Aquarius: home, family, mother

The Dragon's Head will be in your Tenth house of luck, opportunities and growth.

The Dragon's Tail will be on your Fourth house of restructure, karma and change.

Those born in November are going through changes, restructuring in the home and career areas. With this Dragon's Head and Tail, a change in job can also bring about a move from your current home and residents. The Dragon's Head brings luck and opportunity in your career, accomplishments and public standing area of your life.

You have Leo in your tenth house and wherever Leo resides it wants you to shine. It also means to run your own show. If you enjoy doing any type of work with performing arts, theatre, acting, working with children, light-worker or teacher, this is the time to do it.

If you desire to do a business out of your home with the wonderful technology of computers, software and social media, this is another opportunity. Perhaps this would require you to remodel or create the space within your home to do it. For others, you might move to have the needed space to start your new endeavor.

Keep in mind that what you do in your career area may not necessarily be what you enjoy in hobby, creatively or service to your community. You have many options throughout your chart. Once you know the keywords, it helps guide you.

Those in November may be fascinated with Investigative work, stock market, metaphysics just to name a few. Go back to the keywords of the November/Scorpio Zodiac section and review.

People born in December

Your Ninth house Leo: higher learning, philosophies, long distance traveling and mental exploration.

Your Third house Aquarius: communication, short distance traveling, expression, siblings and critical thinking.

The Dragon's Head will be in your Ninth house of luck, opportunities and growth.

The Dragon's Tail will be in your Third house. of restructure, karma and change.

For those born in December your ninth and third houses are going through change and restructuring. With the luck of the dragon in your ninth house it will encourage you to explore the world with a much more expanded global view.

If you think in terms of looking at the entire picture, this is what the ninth house provides. Whereas the third house is relevant to snap shot views, concepts, reasoning and critical thinking.

With the Dragon's Tail in your third house of thinking at times can bring about doubts, frustrations or simply not the clearest of thinking.

Instead, it is encouraging you to reach to the ninth house of mental exploration, philosophies on a grander scale and even taking higher educational classes. The other wonderful aspect of the Dragon's Head in your Ninth house wants you to take faraway trips or travel abroad. This is another method to expand your inner horizons, says your ninth house in Leo.

Spiritual journeys are also included in this ninth house as it dwells in the world of spiritual beliefs, (theology). It clearly wants you to get out of the day to day thinking and get more expansive in higher learning's and studies. If you have a desire to publish any articles or books on spiritual, philosophical or theological topics this is a great time to do this.

Leo rules the performing arts, healing arts and light worker industries, so any classes or mental exploration in these areas can be beneficial during this time. Since Leo rules France and Italy, another good time to explore those areas to gain insight into other cultures, beliefs and way of life.

Those born in December are to understand the natural laws as well of those that are man made law. Return to the keywords in the zodiac chapter for December/Sagittarius to see other ways your birth month relates to you.

People born in January

Your Eighth house Leo: Legacy, death and regeneration, corporate money, investments and inheritances.

Second house Aquarius: self-esteem, material possessions, personal money, such as in your bank account.

The Dragon's Head will be in your Eighth house of luck, opportunities and growth.

The Dragon's Tail will be in your Second house of restructure, karma and change.

Those born in January are receiving the wheel of fortune in their legacy area, which is their eighth house. What is legacy? It is those things that are very significant happenings in your life, for example: buying a house, having a baby, writing a book, selling a home or starting a business just to name a few.

In this eighth house it also touches corporate monies, that which comes through stocks, payroll or other inheritances. With this Dragon's Head there can be money coming in, but money going out to either purchase items for a home, car or any other material possessions.

Anywhere you find Leo, it will want you to shine as does your Sun. Leo is receiving the wheel of fortune in your eight house of legacy, so it wants you to shine and pursue legacy endeavors.Leo rules anything to do with performing arts, healing arts and those industries that do light-work. If you are thinking of running or starting any spiritual endeavor, this is a great time to do it.

As with your second house in Aquarius, this is a good time to advance yourself in the world of computers, technology, astrology or any new age endeavor. Even if learning computers for your business, it is a good idea and timing.

Changing months are August and February during this Dragon's Head and Tail influence.

Those born in January generally are detailed and methodically oriented. Whatever they put their mind to, they will and can fulfill it.

People born in February

Your Seventh house Leo: facing the world, contracts, negotiations, mediation, arbitration, marriage partners and business partners.

Your First house Aquarius: self, innate abilities, physical body, image we project to world.

The Dragon's Head will be in your Seventh house of luck, opportunities and growth.

The Dragon's Tail will be in your First house of restructure, karma and change.

Those born in February are receiving the wheel of fortune in their seventh house of business partners, marriage partners, agreements, contracts and facing the world. This can bring about new business partners and agreements or contract signing. Also, with this can offer you a new way to face the world either with a new title at work, in business, business venture or through a special hobby that you enjoy. Any work that involves promoting knowledge, wisdom, light-work or information to help another is highly encouraged here.

Being born in February already informs you that you are the water bearer, or knowledge bearer through the symbol given to this sign. Any work in computers, electronics, aeronautics or new age endeavors is yours to shine with.

With the Dragon's Tail sitting in your first house it wants you to bring out all those innate gifts and abilities and utilize them. Also to make sure you are taking care of self and health. Physical well-being and self all reside right in your first house.

For those who are single and born in February this can bring about love partners and/or if dating for some time, this can offer marriage during the new Dragon's Head and Tail influence.

For those born in February and are married, this can bring about a new way of relating in your marriage. Leo likes the feeling of being treated like royalty i.e. Queens and Kings. Nothing like going to a day spa and being pampered, followed by an evening at a Broadway show. These are all Leo energy and characteristics.

Be mindful and watch the moon cycles of new moon to full moon when signing these contracts and agreements. Also check to see if there is any Mercury retrograde.

People born in March

Your Sixth house Leo: co-workers, working environment, service to the world, health.

Your Twelfth house Aquarius: subconscious. emotional blocks, hidden from awareness, accumulation of subconscious memories.

The Dragon's Head will be in your Sixth house of luck, opportunities and growth.

The Dragon's Tail will be in your Twelfth house of restructure, karma and change.

Those born in March will be going through changes, opportunities and restructuring in your sixth house of service to the world and your twelfth house of subconscious.

For those working in any capacity, employee, volunteer or as hobbies, could bring change within your work environment as it relates to co-workers or other people assisting in the efforts. Since Leo is a sign that works with children, light-workers, performing arts, healing arts or artistic endeavors, these are encouraged areas to explore.

For the adults, if you really enjoy painting and art, the new craze is wine and canvas parties. This is one of many ways this type of energy is affecting your sixth house. Learning and training in it as a community service, job, or hobby. The choice is yours.

What is also encouraged with this change is to begin journaling your night dreams and writing out your goals. Notice any patterns in dreams, reactions to situations.

Your twelfth house of subconscious is receiving the Dragon's Tail and may want to bring up old patterns, habits or those things that may have been hidden from your awareness to work on. Time to clean out the old it says and bring in the new and more joy. The joy and newness can come from your sixth house in Leo as mentioned.

Since Leo likes to be the king and queen of the zodiac in a humorous sense, treat yourself to some pampering at a day spa. The sixth house references your daily health regimen, so treat that area of your life with goodness and greatness.

People born in April

Your Fifth house Leo: love, romance, children, creativity private entertainment.

Your Eleventh house Aquarius: friends, original experiences, hopes, wishes and dreams.

The Dragon's Head will be in your Fifth house of luck, opportunities and growth.

The Dragon's Tail will be in your Eleventh house of restructure, karma and change.

With the Dragon's Head in your fifth and Tail in the eleventh house, there will be restructure, opportunities, growth, change and challenge.

Those born in April have the wheel of fortune in your fifth house of creativity, romance, private entertainment and your offspring. This is giving you the green light to be creative. Wherever you have Leo/Sun it wants you to shine.

Remember, you are born in April; you have leadership skills and warrior adaptability. This is the general rule, unless you have an afflicted or negative influence happening in your chart, whether by birth chart or current influence. If you are wanting to start a family, you are receiving luck in the area of offspring.

Having Leo in this Fifth house, any work or help with children of the world or your own is highly encouraged. It's even further emphasized as you have now received the Dragon's Head or luck in this area. Field trips with kids or helping children explore through the performing arts, museums and science industries are just to name a few ways to use your fifth house.

If you are not married, a possibility of a romance partner coming into the picture. Look for those born in August. If you are currently married, this is a good time to enjoy some Leo entertainment and romance. This includes Broadway shows, performing arts, romantic dinners or travel to France and Italy for summer vacations.

This Dragon's Head and Tail are giving you an opportunity to be creative, use your genius gifts that come from your Aquarian energy in your eleventh house of wishes, friends and original experience.

Aquarius has anything to do with offering knowledge to your peoples. Computers, new age endeavors, information technology, humanitarian efforts or teaching. I would encourage you to go back and look at the keywords for Aquarius/Uranus in the Zodiac chapter and see what really interests you. Look for those born in February to assist in any of these endeavors.

People born in May

Your Fourth house Leo: home, family, foundation, Mother.

Your Tenth house Aquarius: career, public standing, achievements, awards.

The Dragon's Head will be in your Fourth house of luck, opportunities and growth.

The Dragon's Tail will be in your Tenth house of restructure, karma and change.

Those born in May will be going through changes with regards to home, family, career and personal accomplishments. This includes literal or figurative changes within the foundation of the home. Some people do remodeling on their homes, while others with this change, move to a new home.

If you are deciding to start a business out of your home there is luck on your side with that. Having the Dragon's Tail in the tenth house of career and public standing can restructure you within your current job or a new job and location.

This Dragon's Tail in your tenth house of career and public standing can also encourage you to do something completely different from times past. Since the tenth house is Aquarius, any concepts, ideas or work that is of new age concepts, humanitarian efforts or innovative ideas is highly encouraged.

If you consider yourself a guru or an expert in a field, it is time to share this knowledge with others. Aquarius symbol is that of the person pouring knowledge from the vase. This means sharing knowledge with your peoples.

Whether you use your tenth house as a volunteer, hired employee or self-employee, it all applies. Choice is yours in how you want to use your fourth house of Leo and tenth house of Aquarius.

People born in June

Your Third house Leo: communication, short distance traveling, expression, siblings, critical thinking.

Your Ninth house Aquarius: higher learning, philosophies, long distance traveling, mental exploration.

The Dragon's Head will be in your Third house of luck, opportunities and growth.

The Dragon's Tail will be on your Ninth house of restructure, karma and change.

Those born in June will have changes, opportunities, challenges and restructuring in their house of critical thinking and expression as well as higher learning, mental exploration, philosophies and traveling. It's a great time to be learning something new, especially as it pertains to communications, sales, writing, reading, radio, publishing and any forms of creative expressions.

Traveling short distances or even far away locations can be beneficial to the areas of higher learning and advancing your knowledge in the areas that excite you. Taking classes whether online, in person or from a book is a good time with this Dragon's Head and Tail.

Being born in June your mind tends to want intellectual stimulation, unless you have a negative affliction or a set of planets that encourages you to be more quite and reserved. Doing two things at one time can be quite normal for you. You can be working, traveling and taking a class at the same time.

For those born in June have many gifts to utilize. They have gifts of writing, sales, radio and communications. This is the general rule. It would be good to read the chapter on keywords for Gemini.

So the Universe does ask you, what were you doing 18 years ago as it pertains to your creative expression and mental exploration? What have you learned in 18 years when it comes to your personal philosophies, theologies and spiritual belief systems?

People born in July

Your Second house Leo: self-esteem, material possessions, personal money as in your bank account.

Your Eighth house Aquarius: Legacy, death and regeneration, corporate money, investments, inheritances.

The Dragon's Head will be in your Second house of luck, opportunities and growth.

The Dragon's Tail will be in your Eighth house of restructure, karma and change.

Those born in July are receiving the wheel of fortune, or Dragon's Head in your second house of money, self-esteem and personal possessions.

Therefore these two houses, or areas of your life will offer restructuring, challenge, change and many opportunities to advance you. With this combination of Dragon's Head and Tail positions it can offer you many opportunities with regards to your legacy area. Some examples that touch the legacy area are buying a new home, selling a home, new business endeavor, investments, recalibrating your retirement portfolio and many other things that touch your overall life and legacy.

Since the Dragon's Head is touching the house of money such as your bank account, this indicates that money can be coming in, but at the same time going out to handle the legacy changes. As indicated in the keywords chapter, this can be anything with real estate, chefs, restaurants and hotels just to name a few.

The question to ask yourself is what were you doing 18 years ago? What changes if any was happening at that time in your life? It is a great time to review what has brought you to this moment.

Changing months with this Dragon's Head and Tail happen during the months of August and February. This also includes the month that this change goes into affect, which is April 28th, 2017. Otherwise look to August and February.

CHAPTER 10

Forecast: Saturn in Sagittarius

Written: December 22nd, 2014
December 23rd, 2014 - December 19th, 2017

Saturn Keywords:
Restructure
Task Master
Master Teacher
Disciplined
Karmic Teacher
Father Time
Government
Anatomical: Bones, Teeth and Skeletal System
Location: England

Sagittarius Keywords:
Law Enforcement, Police
Religious, Spiritual Institutions
Religious, Spiritual Leaders
Higher Learning, Education
Schools
Philosophy
Animals, Horses, Vets
Journalists, Journalism, Writers
Photographers, Photography
Sales persons
Newspapers and Publishing
Shamans
Native American Indians
Mental Exploration
Long Distance Traveling
Anatomical: Hips, Thighs, Lower Back
Location: Australia, Spain and Portugal, Southwest US Desert locations

It takes 29 years for Saturn to come back to a sign in its full revolution. Last time Saturn was in Sagittarius: November 16th, 1985 through February 13th, 1988.

By looking at the keywords you can combine some of the Saturn words with the Sagittarius words and can see there will be a complete and full restructure where it comes to law enforcement workers, laws itself and departments. The question will be what is working and what is not?

There will be major changes in our higher learning and educational systems. Whether that is loans for college or new ways of learning methods. This could either make it easier to get a higher education or much more difficult. Are there stricter laws to enter into a school? This is what Saturn and Sagittarius is capable of doing.

A restructure in the publishing, newspaper and journalism fields with regards to the institution itself or the laws that govern these job titles.

Laws or internal changes within religious organizations, seminaries and their leaders are highly probable during this combination of astrological signs.

We may see some changes with regards to animal laws and veterinary medicine or hospitals.

There is an old philosophy; that which is outdated must be leveled and rebuilt. This applies to what is written above. Some circumstances, events or situations create a potential for change, restructure and or rebuilding.

As mentioned in the Keywords for Saturn, Karma! This word weighs heavily here. Meaning, what we are putting into something is what we are getting out of it.

The question to ask yourself is: What have you learned since the last time Saturn was in Sagittarius? How did it affect you? Was it in your career area? Home Area? Marriage? Etc.

Locations such as England, Las Vegas, Palm Desert, Palm Springs, Australia, Spain and Portugal may also go through major law changes and restructuring within their government systems.

Saturn Retrograde: Begins June 14th, 2015 and goes direct on September 17th, 2015.

CHAPTER 11

Forecast: Uranus in Aries

Uranus in Aries: May 27, 2010 - May 15, 2018

Written: June 6th, 2010

To awaken, advance and bring the human race forward

Retrograde note: Uranus will begin its retrograde motion from Aries back into Pisces. It will re-enter Pisces on August 13th, 2010. From August 13th, 2010 to March 11th, 2011. Then forward motion in Aries March 11th, 2011 and then exits May 15th, 2018

What area of your Birth Chart is the new age planet of Uranus in Aries residing now?

Keywords for Uranus/Aquarius/February

Technology
Electronics, Computers, Internet
Aeronautics, Aviation, Defense, Astronomy, Astrology
Geology, Genetics, New Age products
Physics, Time, Space, Energy, Matter, Ley Lines
Telescopes, Microscopes

Jobs/Careers
Scientist, Physicist, Astronomer, Mathematician
Engineer, Information Technology, Electrician
Humanitarian, Teacher (especially New Age), Inventor
Astrologers

Places/Geography
Japan, Ley Lines, the Grid

Things
Inventions, Patents

Health/Body
Electrical components of body, especially heart
Seizures

Environment
Earthquakes, Tsunamis, sudden movements
Volcanoes, Eruptions, Explosions
Hurricanes, Tornados, Lightning
Electrical Storms, Solar Flares

Characteristics
Eccentric, Genius, Intellectual, Pioneers
Think outside of the box, New Age
Independent, Freedom Oriented
Indigo, Autistic tendencies
Panic attacks, Anxiety/Anxious
Abruptness

Keywords for Aries/Mars/April

Technology
Guns, Bullets
Explosives, Fireworks, Fire
Knives, Steel
Atomic Bombs, military weapons

Jobs/Careers
Military, Leaders/Commanders
Steel industry, Building Demolitions
Football, Boxing (contact sports)
Car racing, Stunt doubles
Psychology, Sports psychology
Action movie actors or actresses
Hunters

Things
Race cars

Characteristics
Warriors, Entrepreneurs
Competitive, Head strong
Accident-prone

Health/body
Head, Eyes, Nose, Brain
Sinuses, headaches
Aneurysms, strokes (cerebral vascular accidents)

Places/Geography
Germany

Environment
Nuclear testing sites and facilities

It is important and relevant to understand some of the keywords of each zodiac sign and its governing planet. When reading these keywords you can capture the essence and meaning of each one. Then you can combine a keyword from each category and understand its potential in ones own Birth Chart. The stars do not discriminate against anyone or anything. Our stars in our Birth Chart offer each of us an opportunity to use them to the highest good for mankind and ourselves.

Choice is then given to the "Soul" in how it wants to use any of these energies/properties. For example, for those who have a lot of Aquarius in their Birth Chart, this may offer the soul a great deal of high intellect and a possible gift of a "genius" mind. The question becomes to that soul, how will you use this mental gift? Is it to the betterment of mankind or destroying mankind?

Combining the keywords also offers us information with respect to other areas of interest, such as technology, environment, health, medical and other topics that affect us globally.

Technology

With respect to technology, we can see advancement in the areas of computers, transportation systems, aeronautics, satellites and other hi-tech equipment. Uranus rules the sign of Aquarius, which is all about new age, futuristic ideas, concepts and theories.

Another topic of discussion will be about the functionality of our Grid system. There will be more theories and ideas on how to utilize, update or how to work with our grid system over the next 8 years.

Hi-tech weapon advancement will also take place with this Uranus/Aries combination. Some examples are in the areas of robotic technology, advanced cameras, explosive materials, planes, bombs and other similar weaponry for our Military institutions.

Career/Jobs

All the career areas mentioned in the keyword section will go through major technological changes and advancements.

We will see quantum leaps in technology and equipment over the next 8 years. We think every day that we wake up, yesterday's technology automatically seems antiquated. This will only increase and intensify. Just when you thought you learned something new, think again, it is outdated.

On a positive note, those who work in the medical and computer sciences industries may reap the benefits of the Uranus/Aries combination. This also includes Electrical Engineering and Aerospace industries.

Health/Body

There will be an influx or more than usual amount of people having strokes, aneurysms, seizures and those types of medical circumstances. At the same time we may see more medicines and modalities in preventing or alleviating these conditions. This illustrates how the energies of the stars can be used, i.e. for the good of mankind and modern medicine.

Uranus in Aries combination can or will raise our consciousness level to a much higher vibrations. It has been documented that the Earth is speeding up faster and faster. The "Schumann Factor/Resonance" measures the Earths pulse and vibration. The vibration had registered 7.8 Hertz (Hz). It is said that this 7.8 Hz has been this way for hundreds, perhaps thousands of years. Since around 1980 it has begun to increase and now measures approximately 11 to 12 Hz. There are some theories that by the year 2012 it may be around 15 Hz.

So with this said, we may see an increase in Energy Medicine utilized more. Also more discussions and articles published on these related topics. When Massage Therapists talk about grounding themselves before a therapeutic session with a client, this is where they utilize the Earth's vibration. They attune themselves with the "heart beat" or vibration of the Earth. They do this by telling their mind, body and spirit to harmonize with that same frequency. Give the mind/body directions and it will follow the command.

Places/Geography

Japan (Aquarius) and Germany (Aries).

These areas will go through changes, some of which can be technological, environmental and military.

Because Aquarius/Aries rules earthquakes, explosions, fires, volcanoes, tsunamis- these areas mentioned can be more prone to this energy influence.

Environmental

Weather will be more intense with respect to electrical storms, volcanoes, tsunamis, tornados and earthquakes. This also means with a greater intensity for any of these natural phenomena's.

There will be more books, information and knowledge on Ley Lines and our electrical grid.

One specific area that will need to be watched more closely for Earthquakes is Japan and areas in which are surrounded by water i.e. Indonesia, Philippines, etc.

Some people think Full Moons are triggers for earthquakes. The New Moon applies to this phenomenon as well.

Political

Some people believe that history repeats itself. Similar circumstances, yet different year or era is how it is expressed. It is important then to look for these cycles, patterns and themes. The clues are there. All we need to do is look back into time and determine what took place and when.

Last date Uranus in Aries: From April to October 1927, again from January 1928 until May 1934, and from October 1934 to March 1935.

A sample list of what took place during the last Uranus/Aries combination that began in 1927 to 1935. Almost 84 years ago.

Stock market crash 1929

The United States and Europe were in an economic crisis.

Military were increasing their power in Germany, Italy and Japan.

Japan and China went to war.

Unrest built up and which ultimately led to World War II.

First Transatlantic phone call from US to London

8.6 Earthquake in China that killed 200,000 people

Charles Lindberg flies solo direct from New York City to Paris as the first solo transatlantic flight.

Amelia Earhart becomes first woman to pilot an aircraft across the Atlantic Ocean.

Alexander Flemming discovered Penicillin in 1928.

Adolf Hitler declares himself the Fuhrer Of Germany after becoming President and Chancellor August 2nd, 1934.

The luxury liner Queen Mary is launched in Scotland. 1934

The Securities Exchange Act passed, Securities Exchange Commission (SEC). 1934

The People's car (Volkswagen Beetle) is launched in Germany

CHAPTER 12

Forecast: Neptune in Pisces

Written/Updated on March 12, 2017

April 5th, 2011 to March 30th, 2025

Keywords for Neptune/Pisces/March

Technology
Cinematography
Oil rigs
Boats, Ships and Vessels

Job industry/Careers
Oil industry
Pharmaceuticals
Oceanographers, Navy
Beer and Wine industry
Musicians, Artists, Painters
Piano players
Hospitals, Psychiatric Facilities
Insane Asylums
Cinematography, choreography
Psychics, mediums and intuitive
Magicians, Mystics
Soap Operas, actors, actresses

Priests, Ministers, Nuns, Clergy,
Spiritual workers
Fisherman (This can be the Zodiac sign of Cancer too)
Charter boats
Subconscious, Hypnotherapy

Things
Cruise Liners

Characteristics
Active Imagination
Non-committal, Indecisive
Day dreamers
Artistic, Musically inclined
Creative and Crafty

Health/Body
Feet
Water/fluids in body

Geography
Middle East, Hawaii, Guam
Bodies of water

Environment
Waterways

Places
Theme Parks
Churches, Synagogues
Jails
Hospitals

Religion
Christianity

What is very interesting is when you see a planet that is residing in its own sign. Here we have Neptune, which already governs the sign of Pisces. It amplifies the energy. What is exciting about each sign is the characteristics and elements that each zodiac and planet offer. How wonderful to have magical, mystical and musical all coming from the world of Pisces.

During this time frame these are the types of things offered to all of us in the world collectively and then individually. Also, it will depend on where they reside in your natal chart to inform you on where these characteristics can be utilized or tapped.

Neptune in Pisces is offering all of us an opportunity to expand in spirituality and divine consciousness endeavors. We may see more of the meditation classes or being encouraged globally for all people to counter stress or for overall health.

Another profound advancement, which may be ancient use, is how music is used as a healing modality. Harmonics or vibrational sound healing techniques are being used more now than what I ever knew before. This is a great time to explore these modalities. Music may come way into the forefront during this time frame to be used for many types of situations. There are YouTube videos out now that show people who have not spoken in years, but will respond to the music of their time or era.

You can see in the keywords that Oil is mentioned. Swings on the stock market with regards to oil or highly discussed in the media. The question becomes, does this combination of Neptune in Pisces offer us more of another creative way to use oil, a substitute or new method for energy purposes?

When these influences return from the last time they were combined like this, offers us an opportunity to reflect and reexamine how we were or have used them. We can look back at how our ancestors chose to express their religion, spirituality or means and methods to enlightenment.

Another element of Pisces is imagination. It's interesting to know that Ron Howard, the film producer, is born in March/Pisces and owns "Imagine Entertainment"? He produced many movies, one of them called The DaVinci Code, referencing religion and spirituality; a story of a bloodline of Jesus and Mary Magdalene. Ron Howard's imagination, creativity and art are all noticeable in his movies.

Albert Einstein was born in March/Pisces. Highly creative, genius and imagination to do what he did. I must emphasize, his Dragon's Head and lucky planet of Jupiter resides in the sign of Aquarius. All new age technology, patents and inventions. To read his life story, really explains many facets of his Natal chart. He used his gifts and abilities quite well, and actually started his career in the Patent Office.

The last time Neptune was in Pisces was within a few years after the planet of Neptune was discovered. Neptune moved into Pisces in 1849 and remained until 1862. This information is important to be able to look back in our history and ask ourselves what was happening at that time regarding religion and spirituality? Where have we progressed or regressed? Maybe the answer is both. These answers will be clearer to us as we approach March 30th, 2025.

CHAPTER 13

Forecast: Pluto in Capricorn

Written: July 21, 2007

Pluto in Capricorn: Jan. 26, 2008 - Apr. 15, 2023

The last time that Pluto was in Capricorn was from 1762-1778.

Note: What is written below were my forecasting and predictions for the current Pluto in Capricorn from January 26th, 2008 to April 15th, 2023, written on July 21st, 2007. Does history repeat itself?

Pluto keywords:
Death, Rebirth, Regenerate
Sex and Sex Organs
Legacy
Secrets, Jealousy, Resentment
Metaphysics
Doctors, Surgeons
Criminologist, Detective
Private Investigators
Insurance Companies
Corporate Money
Inheritance, Retirement plans
Stock market, Taxes, Lawsuits
Police Officers
Fanaticism

Extremes
Transform
Eliminate
Purge and Redeem

Capricorn keywords:

- City Hall Workers
- Police Officers
- Public Officials
- Public Service
- Architects
- Political Fundraisers
- Hardware Engineers
- Structural Engineers
- Psychologists
- Governors
- Government
- Organizers
- Detailers
- Antiques
- Ancient Artifacts
- Home Builders
- Circuit Boards
- Life Organizers

Generation Identification explanation: When Pluto enters a sign it has many different meanings. "Generation Identification" happens to be one of the most important meanings. Everyone at one time or another has mentioned their age generation group. Some were born during the baby boomer generation, for example. Using a keyword from Pluto is Birth/Regenerate and for Leo it is Children. Therefore, with this combination of key words, we arrive at baby boom generation.

Thus, the traditional interpretation of generation groups is the same, except that we are using astrology.

Pluto in Capricorn Generation

This is the generation that is going to change government laws when they come into power. Coming into power in this sense is after one has finished their education and started their lives and careers.

The areas of change in government are as follows: local, city, state and then the broader forms of government. They will hold the government accountable for its words and actions. Their mantra will be something similar to "We The People".

In movies we have seen where people storm the White House and bang on their front doors screaming for justice and fairness. Others find themselves at their local city offices demanding to be heard for other inequities. This generation will have zero tolerance to abuse of power or corruption of any kind. Anyone who has fallen through the cracks and has gone unattended to their needs, this generation will speak for them.

If this generation was in power today, hurricane Katrina survivors would have this group to give them a voice. They would use their "generation collective group" to make a difference. The key point here would be that their voice would be loud and change would be much swifter than what is happening now. This generation would have policies in place where the needs of the people would not arrive on the slow boat, but rather with a right here and right now manner.

As to what will transpire within these dates for those of us who are in adulthood, will be a restructuring, change and corrections in our local and federal levels of government. It will happen due to intolerance, frustration and a basic sense of an imbalance to justice and power. In short what will happen during this reign of Pluto in Capricorn is that the current generations in power will simply begin the process. Then, when those born after January 2008 and turn approximately 25 years old, there will be change on top of what the current generations have begun. When they get into power, they will no doubt complete the task with intensity like we have not seen to date.

Here are some examples of what we are seeing now. We have Police on tape beating people and abusing their power. This is happening in America and in other countries. We also see how many of our government officials abuse their power and are brought to our attention faster and more often. The day of internet, bloggers and YouTube is perhaps just one of the reasons why we are hearing about these issues in almost real-time.

We have immigration marchers in the streets of our major cities rallying to their cause to citizenship. There are more discrepancies with members of all political parties to our tax system. There has been a slow roar from people across America and abroad for how those in government positions get away with illegal activities and not punished for it.

When Pluto in Capricorn generation gains full power, there will be no hiding behind the alcohol rehabilitation centers after they have perpetrated corruption, rape, or any other serious crimes. So it is "We the people" that are bringing down the hand of justice and holding people accountable for their words and actions. This only intensifies even more when the Pluto in Capricorn generation gets into power.

Geographical Locations affected: Pluto rules Russia. We will see changes in Russia and the United States. However, England will be the most affected by this Pluto in Capricorn.

As noted above, Pluto rules death and rebirth, like a caterpillar to a butterfly and Capricorn was noted as ruling England. With this combination it is very clear that England will go through a major change.

Capricorn rules England. England will go through major changes and restructuring. This includes everything from social, economic, health-care, educational judicial, administrative, theological and philosophical platforms. This could be change in taxes, laws, government policies or even government themselves as a whole. This is based on what has worked and what has not.

Remaining stagnate or thwarted in any society will create unease or even unrest. There is an innate concept in each of us that growth is very important regardless of who you are what country you live in. Spiritualists call this "soul growth". There is also something called a "collective growth", which means every person living on this planet.

The question that tends to arise is how, why and when such changes take place? The truth is, all things have not unfolded or been revealed yet. Circumstances may not have happened as of yet to make such changes. However, as time goes forward, you will begin to see this unfolding of circumstances and then these phases of change will take place. Some changes will be small and others very dramatic.

In terms of the U.S. and after September 11th, 2001; we had to make changes in government policies because of that circumstance and outcome. An entirely new agency called "Homeland Security" was implemented after this horrific tragedy.

So, it is possible since England also had violent attacks that they might need to restructure government to meet that circumstance. This is just examples of possibilities. It also can bring about new government laws because the people simply want things better for themselves.

We, as a collective society have the potential for positive outcomes for changes that benefit everyone. How does that work you may ask? Well it is simple, it is how you think and feel toward a subject matter.

If you feel that whatever changes must take place, to be done in a way that is beneficial to all mankind, that is creating a healthy change and outcome. If it is filled with hatred, threats and so forth, then the outcome will be offered in a hateful and threatening way. This is similar to the laws of attraction. Like begets like. We do have choice remember in how we act, react or respond.

It is the "We the people" mentality versus it is all for me and no one else. Some people operate from an "I" versus a "We" approach. This also includes "in the name of a religion". People take things to an extreme and ultimately there are extreme outcomes.

Unless and until people realize that regardless of race, color, religion or background, it is a "collective we" at all times. We operate under the same stars, live on the same planet and breathe the same air.

Any person who has an extreme thought in any direction will have an unbalanced position in life. That is a Universal law and principle. No excuses, no exceptions and no justification can be used against this principle.

There is a concept called "Zero Point". The basic premise to this concept is too much of anything in any one direction, thought, action, being or believing is considered not balanced. In otherwords, too much food is not good. Over working is not good. Zero Point is in a harmonious state. It is balanced on all sides. Having the mind, body and spirit in balance is zero point. That is our goal as humans is to operate from this point.

In closing, may England and its peoples find zero point.

People born in January:

Those born in the month of January regardless of the day you are born, will receive Pluto, the planet of transformation, sitting upon their first house of self and innate abilities. This is also their house of natural abilities, soul's purpose, karmic fate and outward appearance.

Those born in January will experience constant inner and outer changes with respect to their innate gifts, physical body and how other people view them. Those born in the month of January tend to work hard toward achievements, career, recognition, high social standing and accomplishments. It is part of their purpose to do so. Having Pluto in this first house of Capricorn will bring new potentials, while old ones drift away as they are no longer needed. It is a time called transforming, rebirthing and evolving. In short the word is growth.

Depending on your natal chart, karma and other natal planets, will offer the intensity of how Pluto in Capricorn will affect you. However, for the most part, a rebirth will take place. This is a time for paradigm shifts my Capricorn friends. How you have thought, acted or even reacted will be revised or changed completely. Life experiences and circumstances is what will bring this about. Pluto is there to help that along. For some Capricorns they will start new adventures, others will want a total mind, body and spirit make over and others will need to let go of old stuff and allow their innate gifts to surface and be utilized.

Here is something for you Capricorns to think about. Since Pluto represents secrets, hidden and buried treasures within, this is what could be explored and brought out to the open. It could be a talent, how you feel about yourself and or a real wish that you have always desired to have or do.

Previous history for Pluto in Capricorn

The last time that Pluto was in Capricorn was from 1762-1778. So what was happing during that time frame? Here are some excerpts found on a simple Google Search. Feel free to find different themes or patterns is the key. What I noticed rather quickly was taxation being implemented, slavery mentioned and different types of trades between countries.

18 May 1764 - The British Parliament amended the Sugar Act from a commercial to a fiscal measure, to tax American colonists.

24 May 1764 - Boston lawyer James Otis denounced "taxation without representation," calling for the colonies to unite in opposition to Britain's new tax measures.

21 May 1767 - Townshend introduced taxes on imports of tea, glass, paper, and dyestuffs in American colonies to provide revenue for colonial administration.

5 March 1770 - British troops killed five civilians when they fired into a riotous crowd of demonstrators in Boston. Writing to sympathizers the next day, Sam Adams called the incident 'The Massacre'. In time this became known as the 'Boston Massacre'.

14 May 1772 - In London, Judge Mansfield ruled that there is no legal basis for slavery in England

14 April 1775 - The first public protest against slavery in America was a resolution signed in 1688 by four German Quakers in Germantown, near Philadelphia. It wasn't until nearly a century later that the first anti-slavery organization was formed. Again the place was Philadelphia, and the organizers were Quakers.

18 April 1775 - At the outbreak of the War of American Independence, US patriot Paul Revere rode from Boston to Lexington, warning people as they went that British troops were on their way.

19 April 1775 - By the spring of 1775, relations between the British Crown and the American Colonials had become extremely tense. The British Army was officially responsible for enforcing various government decrees that the Colonials found unacceptable; the Colonials had formed militias and begun to stockpile weapons and ammunition.

14 June 1775 - The United States Army was founded.

1 March 1776 - French minister Charles Gravier advised his Spanish counterpart to support the American rebels against the English.

17 March 1776 - The end of the Siege of Boston. For almost a year, the siege of Boston remained a stalemate. When General Knox brought heavy cannon from Fort Ticonderoga the tide quickly turned in the Americans' favor, and Boston was reclaimed in a bloodless surrender. The British forces and many Tories departed for Halifax NS.

4 May 1776 - Rhode Island declared its freedom from England, two months before the Declaration of Independence was adopted.

Closing statement

First and foremost, I want to thank you for reading this book and taking an astrological journey with me. It's a humbling experience to learn something and then share it with others. As I mentioned in this book, I am excited that I am experiencing a full cycle (circle) moment as it relates to my studies in this method of astrology.

Learning this eighteen years ago, right when the same Dragon's Head was in Leo of my eighth house of life/legacy and second house of self-esteem, possessions and money is truly divine timing. To have the wisdom to recognize this cycle and reflect is a gift. As my friend Marsha would say, that is growth by leaps and bounds.

My hope is that you are able to look at many areas of your life and reflect. Notice these remarkable gifts given to you when you were born. To utilize every sign and luminary as a precious gift and to the greater good of all involved is a privilege.

Until next time my stargazers.

Safe Astrological Journeys

~ Sister Sage

http://www.karmiclaw.com

About the Author

My inquisitive mind over the years has led me to become, for lack of better words, a professional student. My mind would always be asking questions like, how do you arrive at this? How does this happen? Why does that work?

My professional background began in the medical field for many years until I had the experience of massage therapy. Beginning to learn about alternative or holistic medicine was fascinating to me and I wanted to learn more. I became a trained professional massage therapist in early 1994.

This coupled with my medical background, launched me a few years later into teaching massage therapy with anatomy and physiology. This is where more excitement to my brain cells began to formulate. Is that even possible for a professional student? – I'm laughing out loud! This was an amazing introduction about energy work. After all, massage therapy is a hands-on practice. We are energy beings. Right?

My students learned from my teachings how we could walk in a room and notice if someone was in a bad mood. Have you heard the phrase, you could cut the tension of the room with a knife? Can you imagine having someone offer you a professional massage when they are angry? I have experienced it myself. Part of my training with students was how to ground their energies before working on clients and how to release or let go of energy after a therapeutic massage session.

From here, I enrolled in a school that offered degrees that fit my spiritual beliefs and passions. I received my Bachelor of Science in Metaphysics and went onto receive my Masters of Science in Holistic Ministries. Fast forward several more years, I had many personal experiences that will be better explained in another upcoming book in greater and deeper detail. Allow me to briefly share that I went through stage 3 breast cancer and had a near-death experience in 2007.

Through my healing process and the unfolding of my near-death experience, I learned so many things and needed to put it to use. I was called to complete my studies and receive my Ordination as an Interfaith Minister and Ordained as an Interfaith-Interspiritual Cleric and Minister. I own my business Interfaith Ministry Services LLC and am proud to work as an Ordained Interfaith Minister in my community. I began this amazing work in 2011.

I felt compelled to start a Law of Attraction group and named it, "Spiritual Laws, Theories and Practices Discussion Group". I named it this for many reasons. First it goes without saying there are more universal or spiritual laws than law of attraction. As I have shared in the Spiritual Laws group; we have law of karma, law of opposites, law of gravity, law of nature and so many more. These laws apply astrologically too. In addition, I hosted my radio show, "Spiritual Practices."

I am grateful that all my personal, educational and professional background helps me to compose this book by utilizing the wisdom in each of these areas of my life.

www.ingramcontent.com/pod-product-compliance
Lightning Source LLC
Chambersburg PA
CBHW051709040426
42446CB00008B/802